yukismart.com/b/69b496
AF364385
1
2

body

corps

head

tête

face

visage

grow up

grandir

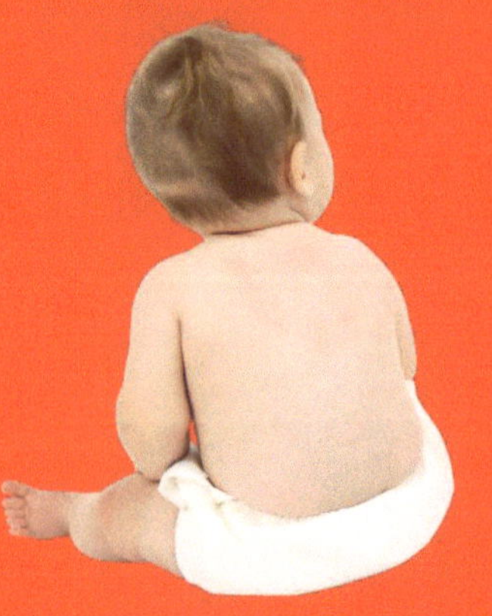

back

dos

chest

poitrine

bottom

fesses

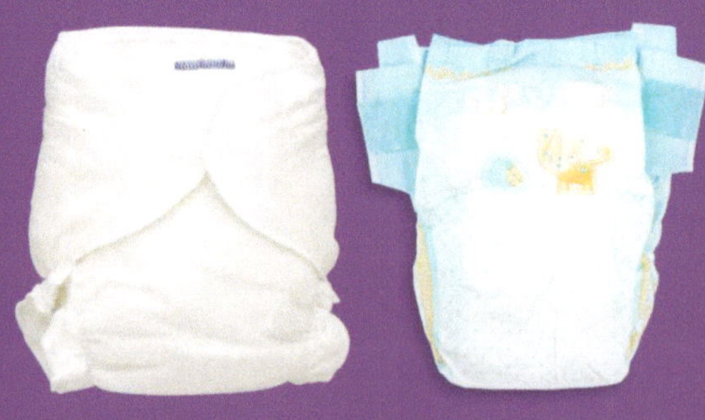

diaper

couche

eye

oeil

glasses

lunettes

forehead
front
chin
menton

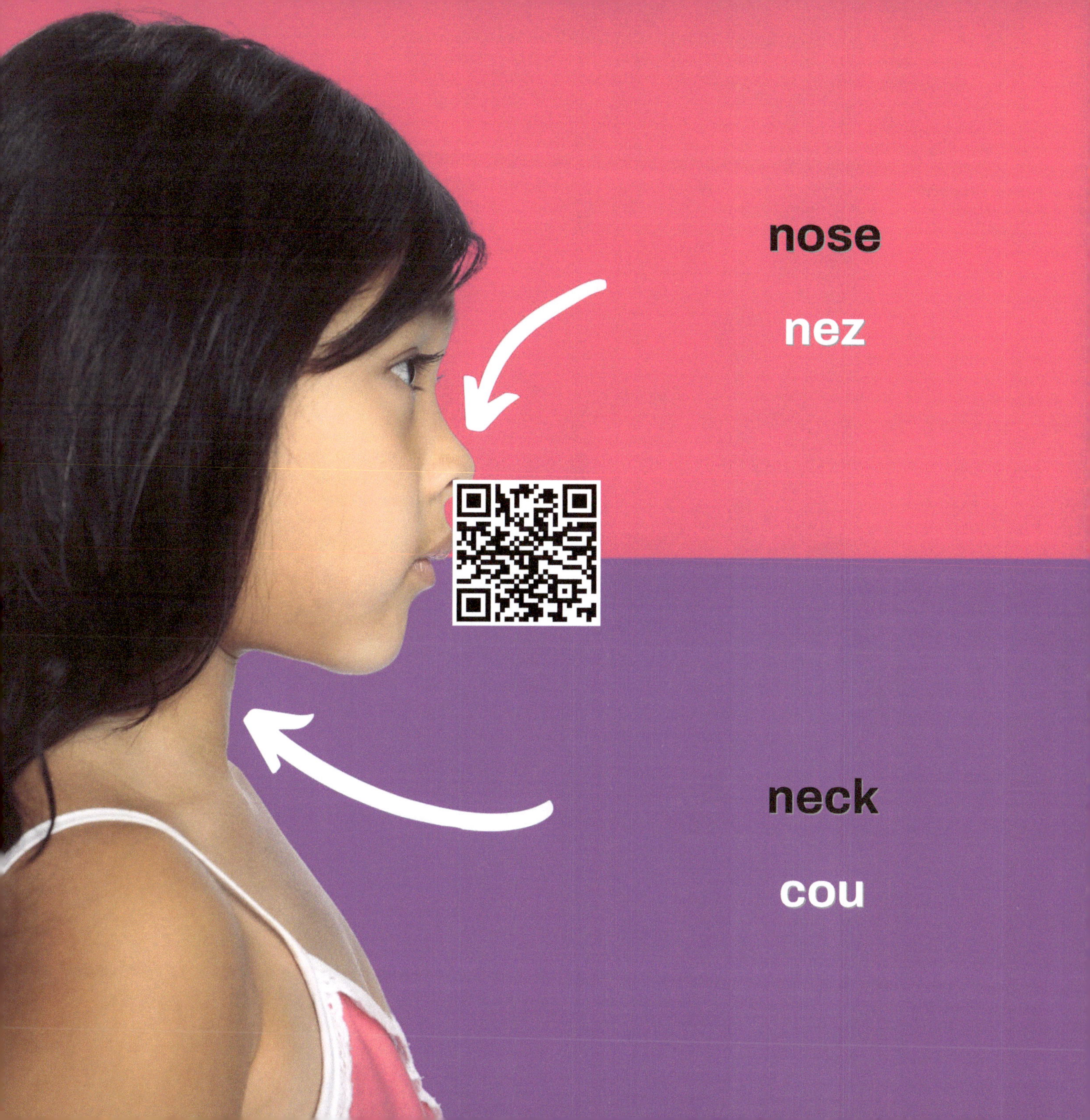

nose
nez
neck
cou

ear

oreille

cheeks

joues

kiss

bisou

mouth

bouche

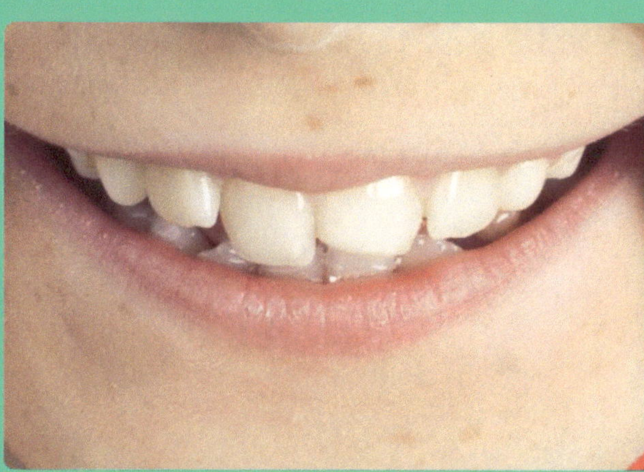

teeth

dents

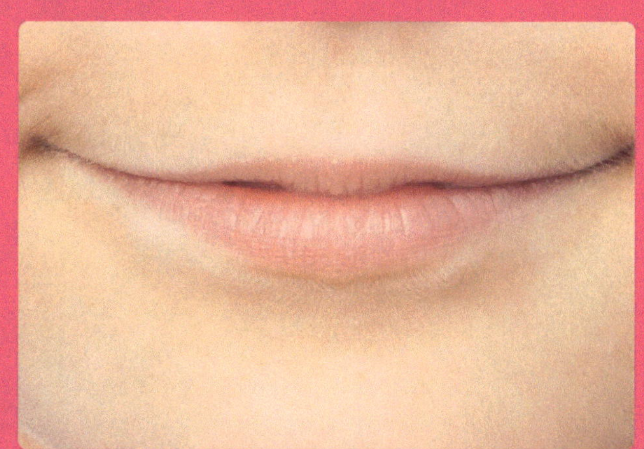

lips

lèvres

tongue

langue

hair

cheveux

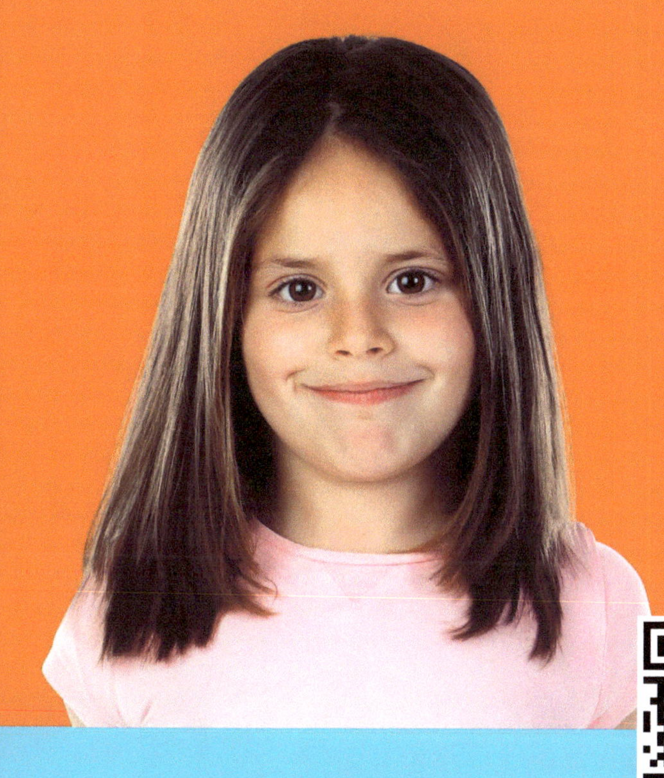

straight hair

 cheveux raides
cheveux droits

curly hair

cheveux bouclés

black hair

cheveux noirs

brown hair

cheveux bruns

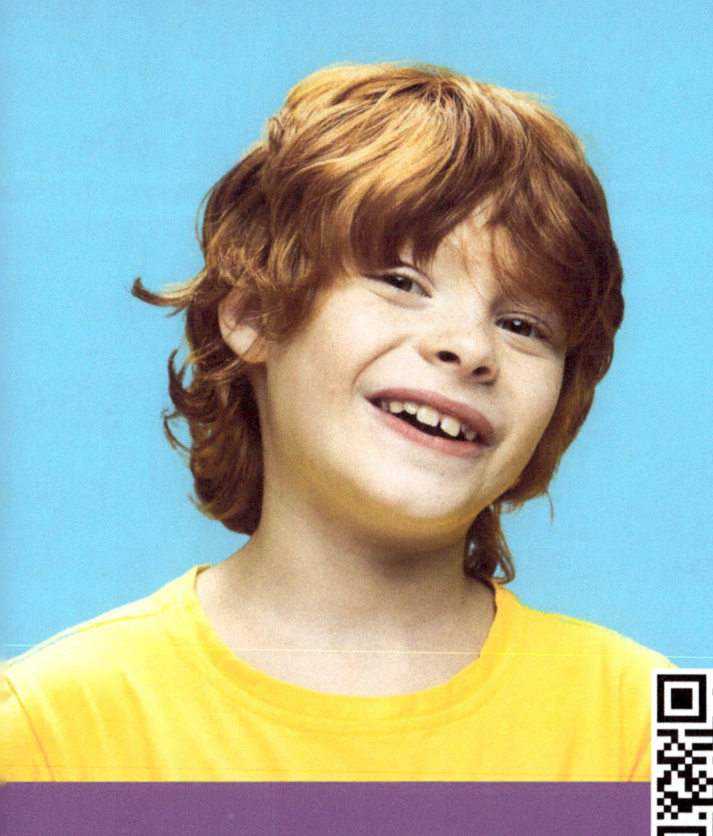

ginger hair

cheveux roux

blond hair

cheveux blonds

gray hair

cheveux blancs

bald head

chauve

beard

barbe

moustache

moustache

arm
bras
elbow
coude

hand

main

fingers

doigts

thumb

pouce

belly

ventre

navel

nombril

foot

pied

leg

jambe

heel

talon

thigh
cuisse
ankle
cheville

calf

mollet

nails

ongles

knee

genou

necklace

collier

hat

chapeau

bracelet

bracelet

scarf

🇫🇷 écharpe
🇨🇦 foulard

coat

manteau

pullover

🇫🇷 **pull**
🇨🇦 **chandail**

pants

pantalon

dress

robe

rain boots

bottes de pluie

socks

chaussettes

shoes

🇫🇷 **chaussures**
🇨🇦 **souliers**

mittens

🇫🇷 **moufles**
🇨🇦 **mitaines**

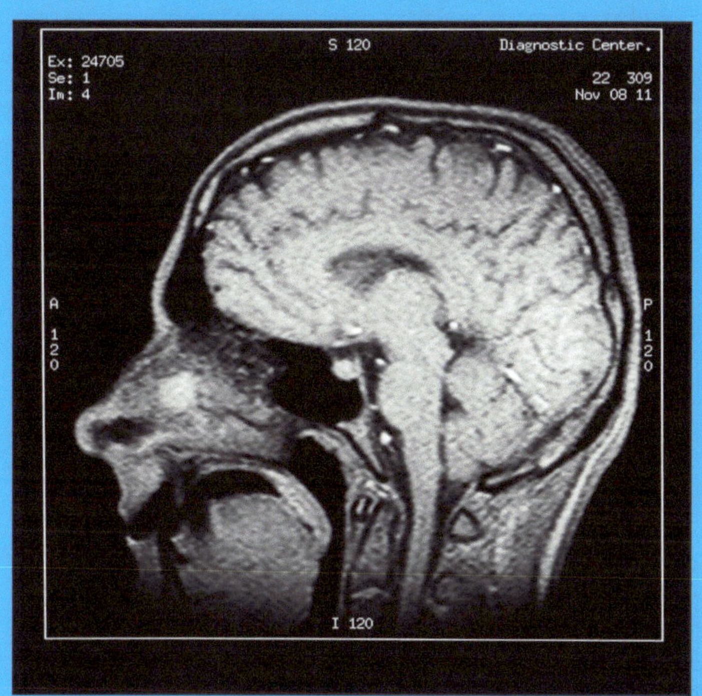
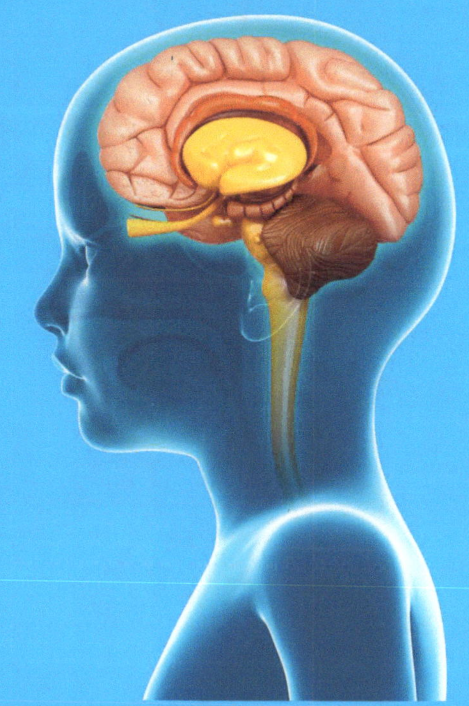

brain

cerveau

heart

cœur

lungs

poumons

skin

peau

sunscreen

crème solaire

sun glasses

lunettes de soleil

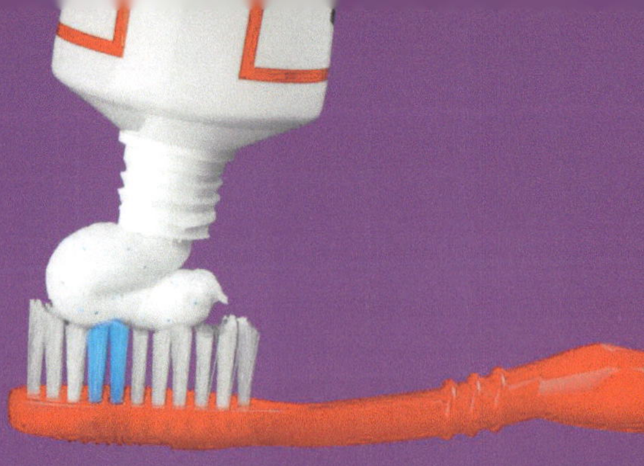

soap

savon

toothpaste

dentifrice

toothbrush

brosse à dents

pain

douleur

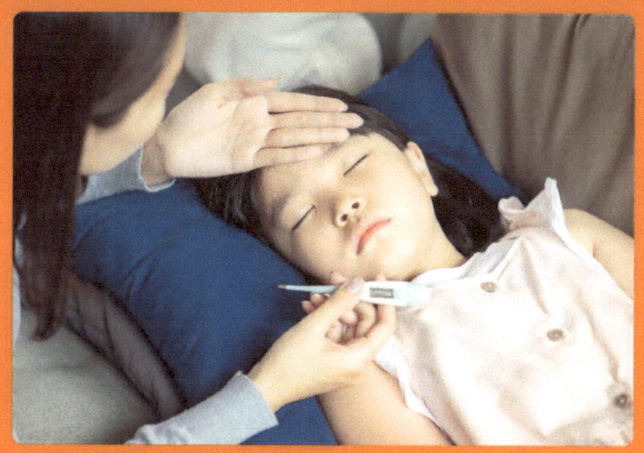

fever

fièvre

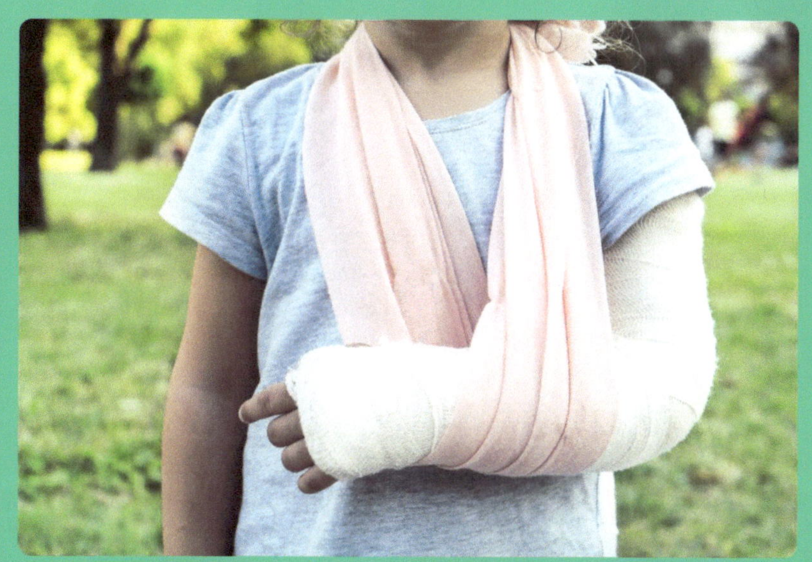

broken arm

bras cassé

sneeze

éternuement

cough

toux

dental cavity

carie

pharmacist

pharmacien

medicine

médicament

hospital

hôpital

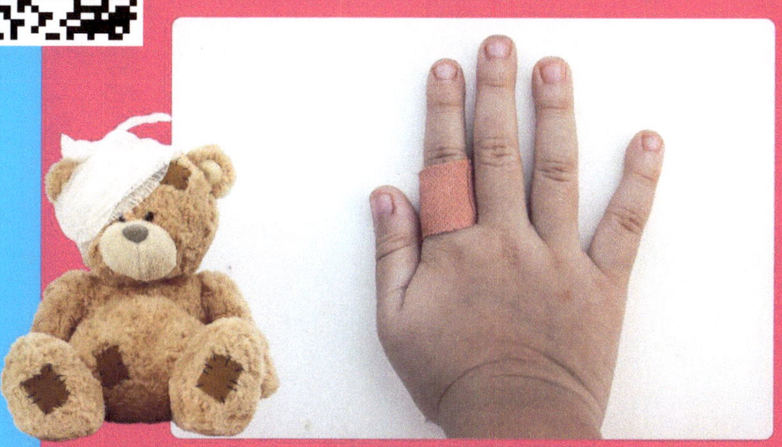

bandage

pansement

paramedic

ambulancier

firefighter

pompier

firetruck

camion de pompier

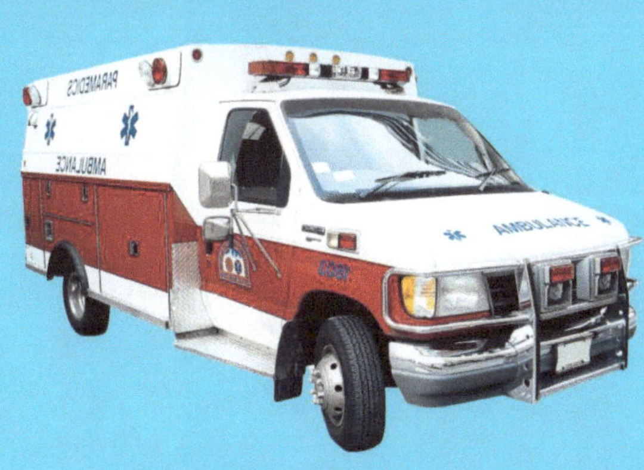

ambulance

ambulance

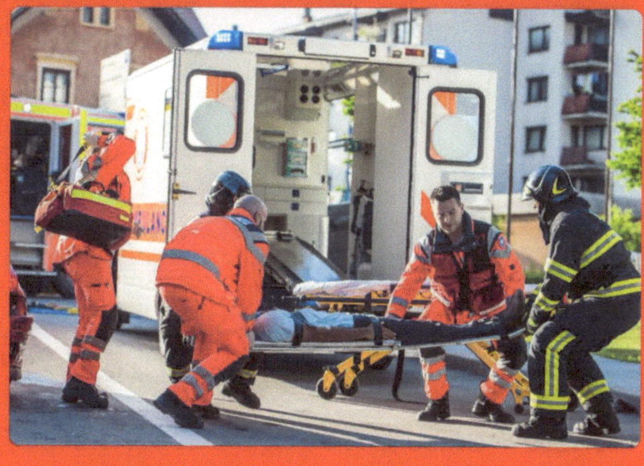

rescue team

équipe de secours

helicopter

hélicoptère

boat

bateau

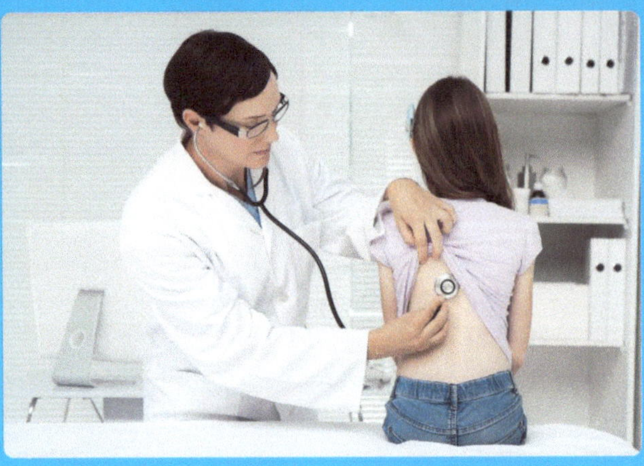

doctor

docteur

nurse

infirmière

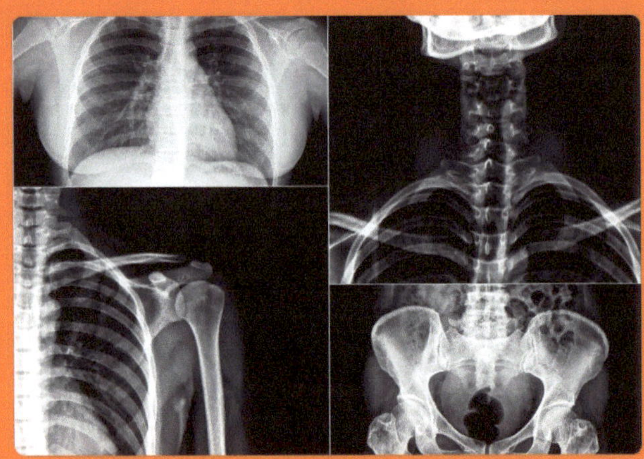

x-ray

radiographie

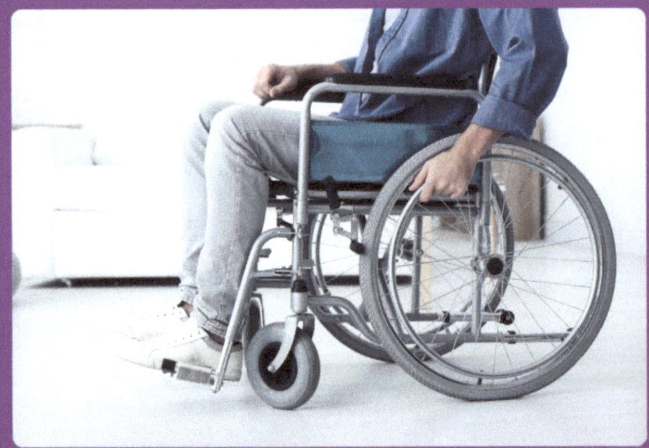

wheelchair

fauteuil roulant

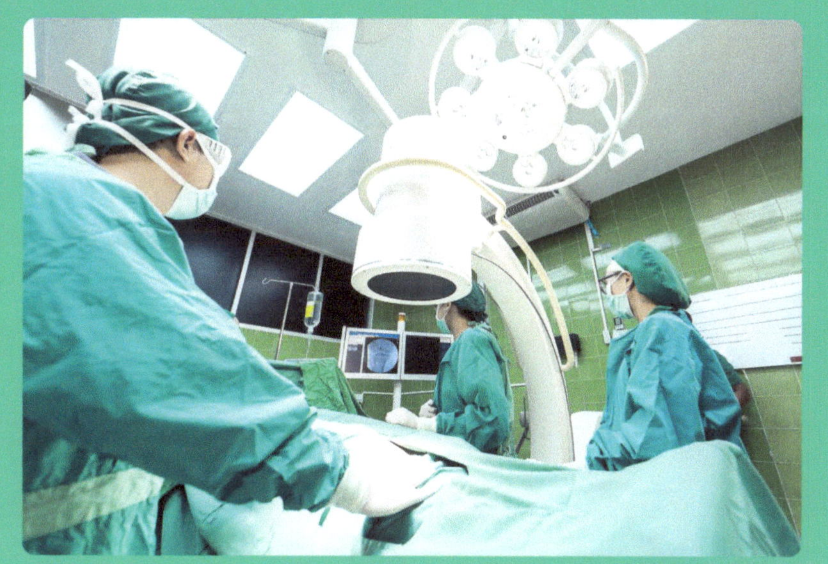

surgeon

chirurgien

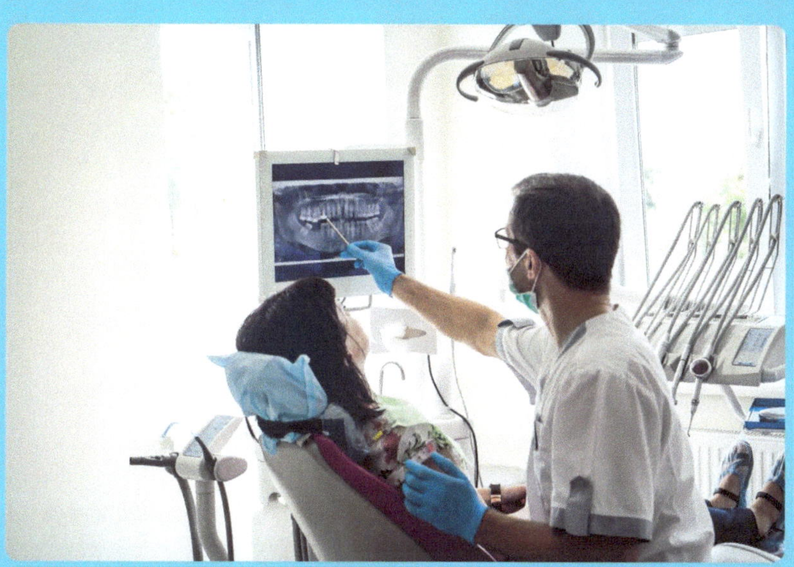

dentist

dentiste

thermometer

thermomètre

scale

balance

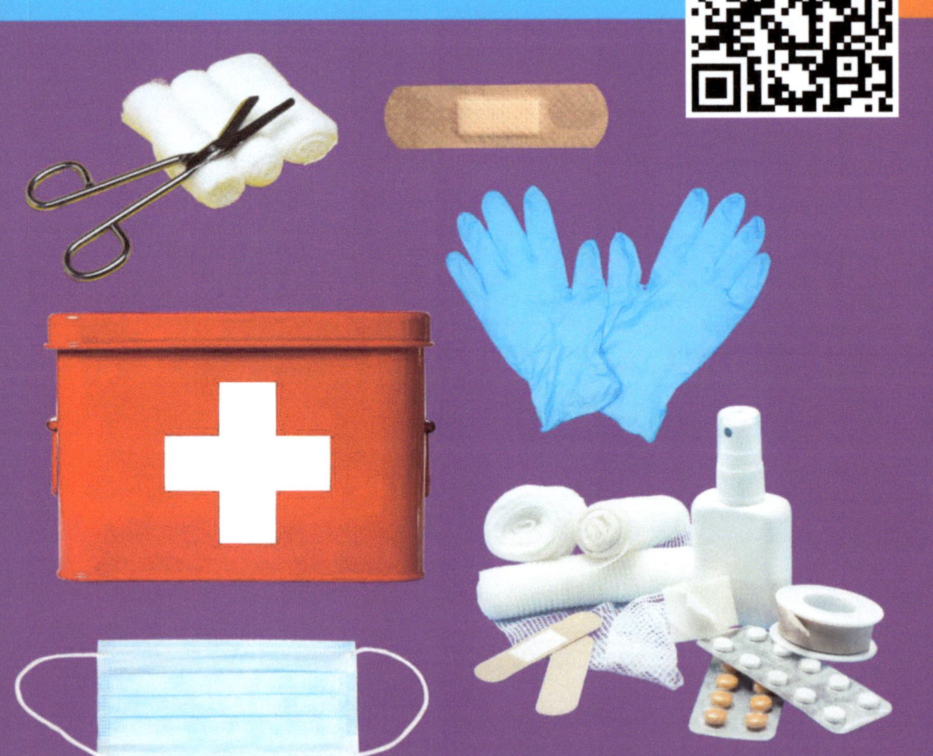

first aid kit

trousse de secours

vet

vétérinaire

stethoscope

stéthoscope

dancing

danse

basketball

basket-ball

soccer

football

soccer

swimming

natation

skiing

ski

judo

judo

9 782384 124879